MAINE

For Brett —

Hope you like these poems.

Best,

Jonah Winter

MAINE

Poems

by

JONAH WINTER

Winner of the 2001 Slope Editions Book Prize

Selected by David Lehman

SLOPE EDITIONS

New Hampshire | New York | Massachusetts

The author gratefully acknowledges the editors of the following publications in which some of these poems first appeared, occasionally in different form:

The Antioch Review: "Homage to William Shakespeare," "The Lord's Prayer in American"
Chicago Review: "Ode on Complexity," "Unrequited Love: A Slide Presentation" (Slides 1, 2, 4, 6 and 7)
Exquisite Corpse: "Hair Club for Corpses," "The Orchid Shop," "Trip to the Salad Bar"
Mudfish: "Soliloquy on Botticelli Ave"
New York Quarterly: "Sestina: My Women"
Northwest Review: "Unrequited Love: A Slide Presentation" (Slides 3 and 5)
Passages North: "Description of the Universe" (1st)
Ploughshares: "Season's Greetings from the Winter Family!," "Sestina: Bob"
Poet Lore: "Amnesia" (4th)
The Quarterly: "Romantic Love, 1987"
Slope: "Sestina: Elk vs. Non-Elk," "Ode to a Nightingale Revisited," "Sestina: A Cowboy's Diary," "Ode to the Brooklyn Zoo"
Talisman: "Art"
Third Coast: "Against Simile," "In the Best of All Possible Worlds," "Ode: Kritique of Pure Reason"
Threepenny Review: "Lines Composed a Few Miles Below The Empire State Building"
Timbuktu: "Amnesia" (1st), "Amnesia" (2nd), "Amnesia" (3rd), "Cowboys and Indians," "Mollusks and Mankind," "Soliloquy Beginning in Anger," "Whoopy Tie Yie Yoe," "Conversation With Inflatable Doll," "Girl Accuses Father of Taping Her Mouth Shut," "December Mosaic"
The Pushcart Anthology 2001: "Sestina: Bob"

The author also gratefully acknowledges the existence of Lord Exister, Lady Rapunza, Little Buddy Bartrum, Johnny Sportcoat, Wildcat Sal, Commissioner(s) Gordon, and Mr. Max.

Published by Slope Editions
www.slopeeditions.org

Library of Congress Cataloging-in-Publication Data
Winter, Jonah.
Maine : poems / by Jonah Winter. — 1st ed.
p. cm.
"Winner of the 2001 Slope Editions Book Prize."
ISBN 0-9718219-2-5 (alk. paper)
1. New York (N.Y.) — Poetry. I. Title.
PS3623.I67 M35 2002
811'.6–dc21

2002012263

Cover design by Ed Miller
Book design by Nate St. Germain
Cover photo by Jonah Winter

Printed in the United States of America

9 8 7 6 5 4 3 2 1

FIRST EDITION

TABLE OF CONTENTS

IV

V

VI

VII

INTRODUCTION

If on a winter's day a traveler…

If a table of contents can function as an index to the poet's sensibility, Jonah Winter's titles give him a head start in the wit department – a phrase I was about to strike when I realized that a cabinet-level department of wit is not a bad fancy with which to commence talking about this fine book.

The table of contents of *Maine* promises "Lines Composed a Few Miles Below the Empire State Building" and "The Lord's Prayer in American" and no fewer than four poems entitled "Amnesia." These titles prepare the reader well for the pleasures that follow. It is the nature of poems to relate to earlier poems as to ancestors, and Winter manages unconventional dialogues with the Wordsworth of "Tintern Abbey" (and with the Keats of the Nightingale Ode) while being fully conscious of the American language and identity that separate him and us from a poetic heritage that remains oceans and centuries away but belongs in some measure to us nonetheless.

There are obvious ways in which poetry calls upon the resources of memory. Less obvious is the affinity that exists between poetry and amnesia, memory's opposite, if only because all memory is selective and therefore involves a certain amount of erasure. Winter's "Amnesia" turns out to be a compelling state to observe if not to dwell in, naturally cinematic, where childhood gets misplaced ("like a paper sailboat"), heroes set records in "Unsuccessful Ideas Carried Out," and the voice saying "I have to do my laundry" vies with the voice out of the *Duino Elegies* declaring that "Every angel is terrible."

I like Winter's conversational drive, his variety of subject matter, and his assertive but wacky voice. There are odes inspired by Immanuel Kant, the Brooklyn Zoo, and the sort of "complexity" that informs any instant in New York City where multiple (almost contradictory) facts must be held in the mind as one crosses a boulevard against the light in the approved New York manner.

Jonah Winter is unafraid to have a good time in his poems, and that is fortunate, because a sometimes overlooked law of poetic composition is that the more fun the writer has, the more fun the reader will have. Winter's sestinas – the "Bob" Sestina, where a single word ends all the poems' lines, a second that uses esoteric teleutons, and a third in the form of a "cowboy's diary" – are very funny. In a sense they test the limits of silliness; on a deeper level they explode the notion that writing in a strict verse form acts as an inhibition or signifies a conservative bent of mind.

You won't have any trouble remembering this *Maine* or recollecting in tranquility the winter's day on which you read it.

David Lehman, 6/1/02

MAINE

Lines Composed a Few Miles Below The Empire State Building

Many of my best friends are Italian.
I don't know why, but anyway
last year a friend of mine who's more acquaintance
than friend, more Italian than acquaintance,
broke my arm. When I told another friend
whose father is Italian, she said her father
knew people who might be able to break the legs
of the guy who broke my arm.
I tried to explain to her, and urged her
to explain to her father that the broken arm
got broken accidentally—nobody's fault—
we were arm-wrestling, and I'm not sure what happened—
I suppose my desire must supersede my strength.
In any case, I told her to tell her father
not to worry, though I did appreciate his concern
and still feel comforted to know that were I to ever,
as it were, "get hurt," by an Italian,
I could enlist the aid of some other Italian.
But these aren't the sort of thoughts I want to be thinking
today, as I stroll along, half-imagining
the limousines to be gondolas, half-perceiving
the Cutlass Supremes and the wispy-thin moustaches
of the teenage boys who drive them,
powering out loud disco beats on sound systems
designed for large dance-halls. What is it
with these second generations? Don't they get
the beauty of their parents' rich European culture?
Is there no marginal survival of tradition?
Does every moment have to be a rough translation
of some other moment, or can't we
keep sitting at the little moonlit table,
our silent thoughts accompanied by the strolling accordionist's
sweet sounds of yore, again and again,
the same waiter handing us the same glass,
year after year, the same absinthe,
the same breeze blowing through the leaves of the pepper tree
until there is not one breath
we haven't breathed before?

I know my soul is most at peace when I
come back to a place I've been before,
even if I can't remember anything
except for a mood, as in Venetian blinds,
the sense of a tradition being made, a religion
very private and unarticulatable,
a woman leaning out of a window
with hardly anything but a towel wrapped around her
not exactly like any sight I've ever seen
and yet enough like certain ones to incite in me
an adoration endless yet complete,
the woman turning into an icon
the moment I envision her, up there
where she will be forever
brushing a wisp of dark hair from her eyes.

In the Best of All Possible Worlds

The kid's finger wouldn't bleed when you slice it,
and the guy who puts the band-aid on wouldn't be a dealer,
and the kid's mom wouldn't be cursing the kid,
and the laundromat attendant wouldn't be shouting stuff
in some other language about the guy who's putting the band-aid on,
nor would the change machine be broken,
nor would the dealer be talking with other dealers about some guy
who got killed on 13th Street,
nor would the guy who got killed be lying in some metal box,
nor would the guy who puts the tag on his foot be sneezing right now,
because it would never be very cold, and so
the man who's standing outside the cathedral would not be wearing garbage bags
and wouldn't have to stand there day after day, in the same spot, and
of course there wouldn't be any garbage bags
because there wouldn't be any garbage,
and so that beer bottle someone just broke outside the laundromat
wouldn't exist,
and neither would beer, since people wouldn't have to drink beer
or take drugs, and so the dealers wouldn't have to sell drugs,
and probably the dealer who put the band-aid on the kid
wouldn't have had to hit that lady in the face right now,
and she wouldn't have had to disrespect him
in regard to the drug deal, nor would the kid
with the bleeding finger be forced to watch this
nor hear the lady say "you fucked up my face"
nor would anyone have to say "fuck" anymore
for the sake of frustration or intimidation,
since no one would ever be frustrated or needing to intimidate people,
so in other words, when I get home from the laundromat,
I wouldn't need to throw stuff out the window
down at the skinheads on the street,
nor would the skinheads need to make all that noise
and wear those spikes around their wrists
and grease up what little hair they have to look scary
nor feel compelled to wear leather jackets that say
"Die Yuppie Scum"
because there wouldn't be any yuppies,
because no one would need to be upwardly mobile,
because everyone would be content exactly where they were,
with exactly the right amount of money in their pockets
to buy a healthy meal and a roof for the night.
But since this is not the case,
we might as well stand at the window and watch
as the limousine with Jersey plates
rolls to a stop by the laundromat
then pulls away nice and easy, just
like a zipper on a body bag.

The Lord's Prayer in American

The hand that picks up the telephone is God.
All spoken words are birth certificates.
Jesus Christ is a thing that happens when you sleep with a person
you've been talking to for hours and hours.
If the bus that's passing by is empty,
if what you had meant to say is replaced
by a waiter taking your order,
that's okay.
These are the nights you have been waiting for.
The woman in the purple tiara has arrived,
bearing a basket of fruit.
Nothing you say can change the smile
painted on her lips curved in speech.
Nothing you say can make the fruit more real
though the apples and bananas are plastic – that's okay.
What starts out an invisible rose
soon ends up a parked car.
Love it or leave it. This is America.
Your chicken-fried steak is not quite ready.
The cook had to take a leak.
If this is not what you wanted to hear,
if what you wanted to hear was
Our father, who art in heaven,
Hallowed be thy name,
I am truly sorry.
I can't remember the rest of it
though I want to believe in everything.
I want to believe that the words coming out of the angel's mouth
are simply a response to a broken umbrella.
I want to believe that the angel's wings
are made of shredded newspapers.
I want to believe that the path to heaven
has an all-night convenience store,
that the guy behind the counter will say good night.

Against Simile

There comes a point when you could just say
the hushed light over the harbor at dawn
is like the padded insoles in a pair of wingtips
is like the marquee flashing on and off
"TONIGHT" is like an artificial heart machine
somehow probably – the tautness of a rope
connecting a boat to the pier
might help you see the curve of someone's body
dividing up the night into rain and flesh
which are so different, really, like canvas awnings
over windows in New England, sometime late in August,
at dusk, when whoever owns the house is outside
drinking gin and tonics at a little white table
while a scruffy little dog sniffs around by the pine trees
bordering the yard – that's a lot different from a switchblade
held at the throat of a woman in an elevator
stuck between two floors of a building in Harlem:
this one moment with the knife is like a candle
held up to a photograph that's like the woman's childhood,
all of it burning away, so quickly, efficiently,
while all the stars above the rooftop continue
to just sit there
like random, distant, non-functional but extremely large rosary beads.

Art

The naked lady's finishing her break, just about to take off
her leather biker jacket – a nice touch –
when this really fat lady in the back (and one of the only ladies) says
"Leave it just like that."

Two or three artistes say "Yes" and nod artistically,
staring at her nipples, perhaps squinting, even,
perhaps tilting their heads sideways
and rearranging their easels to get a better view.

So this poor model, who has an unusually large patch of pubic hair
(you see, I'm an artist too – that's why I notice these details) –
this model has to sit there with this biker jacket
half-way off her naked body:

everyone silently sketching away, very seriously, with classical music,
Vivaldi, I think, playing in the background....
You know, there was a certain time in my life
when girlfriends used to model nude for me.

It would always start out serious and seemingly
with the best of intentions:
The squinting, the measuring, the erasing,
getting the proportions just right.

It would get to where I could almost feel the volume
of her body as I drew it,
the sense of a thigh taking up space,
the roundness, the fleshiness, the 3-dimensionality—

which is when I hurriedly tossed aside all pretense,
leaving, of course, a long jagged line
across my masterpiece, alas unfinished, and, by this point,
utterly useless!

Homage to William Shakespeare

The moment you decide that nothing is deserving
of serious attention, somebody dies,
leaving behind a closet of moth-eaten dresses
or a couple of thousand dollars
or else someone loses the use of his legs
in an automobile accident or has a tumor
or any number of things that one has to work
to milk any humor from, in which case
it's probably safe to say that the subject is basically serious,
warranting an open eye, an alert facial expression
with mouth closed, keeping hands inside pockets
for the duration, nodding from time to time,
shaking one's head at the ground, perhaps remarking
that at such times music is the only mode of expression
worthy of saying what needs to be said though of course one hopes
that language might offer some escape route,
some trap-door backstage through which one might leave King Lear
raging at the helpless audience of dilettantes and pseudo-intellectuals
who've paid outrageous amounts to be amused – by what? –
some guy made up to look old with a phony English accent
while down the street a real Spanish cook is pouring oil
into a huge pan of onions, complaining, in half-English/half-Spanish,
about the transmission to his 1979 Impala station wagon
parked in front of the restaurant, where it broke down but is now
being worked on by three of his friends.

Emergency Preparedness

I knew a man in Texas once whose job was to alert the entire city of Dallas
in the event of some natural disaster like a flood or tornado or even
severe thunderstorm, which in Texas can be pretty severe – for example:
during my father's boyhood next the Katy railroad tracks,

his mother was so apocalyptically concerned about the weather
(one of the many affects of her religious fanaticism/psychosis
which seems to have cleared by the time I showed up on the radar),
she would force the entire family (all 10 of them!) down into the storm cellar

whenever there was any sort of meteorological disturbance which upset her.
Once in the cellar, she would apparently moan and wail, saying unhelpful
things like
"O Lord, we're all gonna die" and "Good Lordy Mercy!"
until the storm had passed (she was the dominant parent).

This behavior system, it must be pointed out, is an aberration in Texas.
But, alas, this acute storm phobia was passed on to my father
(and through some bizarre twist in the nature/nurture rubric, to my late dog
"Polly").
My mother's been pretty understanding, but when he suggested building a
storm cellar

outside their new West Texas home, she drew the line, a line my father paces
nervously
every time the faintest thunder rumbles in the not-so-distant distance.
But I had intended to talk about my friend, the Emir of Emergency
Preparedness,
who appeared on the news any time there were emergencies,

real or potential. The last time I saw him, he was living above his garage,
exiled by his wife who had chosen his birthday to tell him
she was having an affair with another man, probably a man who knew nothing
about what to do in, say,...a monsoon.

Poor Ernie, kicked out of his own house, gaining weight and getting drunk
nightly. I picture him raising a bottle of Rebel Yell
up to his lips, leaning his head back for way too long,
and saying something glib about marriage. We played Irish folk music

once a week back then. I was only 15 and didn't understand
what he was going through. I had no idea what personal disasters
awaited me in the years to come, or the night when, before a group of
strangers
in one particularly gloomy church basement, I would be sharing

my experiences, one by one, as the rain outside
got so loud occasionally that some of the haggard faces would turn
towards the darkened windows, pausing momentarily while I continued
my litany of failed relationships, escapades with gun-toting lesbians,

stints in jail, homelessness, adultery, insanity…
The house I live in now is way up yonder in the frozen north
where snow is the only thing I have to worry about.
But rest assured my shelves are stocked. I am prepared.

Snow White

My first experience of unrequited love was with Snow White
at the age of 5: sitting in my little rocker
I closed my eyes and listened to her sweet voice
sing I'm wishing I'm wishing…on the one I love

which I pretended she was singing to me
as real tears rolled down my tiny cheeks
and onto my little bathrobe, stiff from all the salt
of almost daily crying sessions.

Then, as a coping mechanism I suppose, I transferred
all the love I felt for Snow White onto a little girl
in my kindergarten class, name of Laura, appropriately enough –
a youthful and entirely subconscious nod to Petrarch's heart-break,

that very adult obsession, who, like Gene Tierney in the movie,
only attained more magic through her absence
that ironically attained more presence than her presence
about which we can only speculate.

Skipping ahead 30 years, after a series of bungled love affairs
and mismanaged relationships, passion, ardor, hope
wasted more or less on the wrong individuals
at the worst possible points in all of our tortured lives,

I met another woman named Laura, who, appropriately enough,
was married, lived 3,000 miles from me, and had a thing
for homosexual men which caused her apparently to grab the crotch
of my good friend Robert who is gay.

He told me this story to exemplify how straight women
are always falling for him, just as I fell
for Laura, who naturally blossomed in my heart
to become a snow white princess – a Princess, yes,

whose own pure heart belonged alas to the handsome homosexual
Prince Charming, who shed real tears in my pick-up truck
trying to explain how it wasn't his fault:
this is how it's always been.

If I were writing this screenplay, I'd re-cast the roles:
Robert would be Snow White, Laura would be Prince Charming
and I would be the Old Witch staring intensely
into a full-length mirror that would tell me all those things

I never hear: your hair, so beautiful, your blue eyes
so lovely, etc., etc., while under the lid of the glass coffin
Snow White in drag would undergo a series of wet dreams
observed by Prince Charming, whose female form

would be glistening naked in the moonlight
through the pines, where, panting, struggling in vain
to pry the coffin open with her fingers, so slippery
with sweat that covered her entire body,

she would, in the eleventh hour of her being, discover
who it was she really loved…
At this point, the fat lady with the camera would intervene,
directing us to change roles, start from the top.

II

Unrequited Love: A Slide Presentation

Slide # 1

Here we see a sort of stagecoach irony,
a grim reaper, so to speak, in the foreground,
asking for the lily white hand of a corpse
who, as you can see, does not respond
seeing as how she is hanging out one of the windows
of the little covered wagon which, alas,
will travel no farther this evening.
(The horses stand awake all night, still harnessed
to the reins which have fallen
from the hands of the driver, who is slouched
forward, his hat blown far across a field
pale with moonlight and romance, except
far too many crickets inhabit this landscape,
mosquitoes, chiggers, occasional auto parts.)

Slide # 2

Doves are cooing.
Forsythia blossoms
appear, one by one,
on their stems
as the rain goes on
breaking promises
day in and day out,
town to town,
mannequin to mannequin,
plaster smile to plaster smile
(and here is the little boy who,
walking through a pasture in the fog,
hears the sound of a cow's mooing
but seeing nothing
does not know which way to go).

Slide # 3

You may not be able to make out the stars
in this picture – but they're there;
and probably you can't see the Eiffel Tower
lit up at night – it's there and it's lit;
it might be good, then, to mention all the tulips,
too, cupping the rain, which just stopped
an hour ago, during a magnificent sunset
which, unfortunately, may not here be viewed.
The advantages of total darkness are:
1) Would you like to go to the movies with me?
2) I played baseball in the third grade.
3) E = Mc2.
4) The telephone is ringing.
5) Aren't you going to answer it?

Slide # 4

Instead of viewing this desert as just a desert,
close your eyes, envision an oasis:
it's midnight, the camels are drinking
peacefully in the background, under a moon
that's slowly descending through the fronds of a palm tree
under which the Bedouins are sleeping,
man and woman, arm in arm,
dreaming similar dreams perhaps:
a little boat on the big, big ocean,
the tropical ocean, where flying fish are flying
above the waves to watch the lovers love…
No one in the world knows they are here
except you, and you must keep this a secret.

Slide # 5

You have just three minutes
to tell me everything you know about desire
and it's okay to wear that Spanish hat
but please – the perfume too? I mean
everything and nothing share a room
no larger than a closet in the Bronx
and yet I know they don't sleep together –
the point of what I'm saying is: like me, you probably think
the more you love an object, an umbrella, for instance,
the more it turns into a prayer for rain,
the more the rain forgets what it wanted to say,
what it wanted to say forgetting the importance of a shoe
abandoned in the gutter, the water
rushing in, assuming the shape of a foot.

Slide # 6

Now that I have your undivided attention,
here's a definition of desire:
the thing beyond the thing beyond,
anchor dropped, rope pulled taut
against the waves, vanished hand
on the railing, everything to lose –
how could you possibly walk through a cloud
in a three-piece suit without thinking
"Yes – this is as it should be,
what was translating all into nothing,
the handle the trapeze artist misses
swinging to the other side,
a person turning into a blizzard
with no sign of any travelers."

Slide # 7

Well here's another one of the desert.
Again, it's night; again, there's no one here
and yet, if you listen closely, you may hear
a creature howling in the distance, a slight breeze
lifting up the flaps of the tents
empty now for weeks and weeks…
Is this how we say good-bye
in Swahili? with ukuleles
strumming along in the background
off behind the velvet curtain of indigo
falling, indefinitely, from the stars,
little peepholes into the backstage
party: a tiger
bounding through a flaming hoop.

III

Amnesia

I forget what happens next.
A chair explodes. Someone gets on a bus
for Pasadena. There's a special
on artichokes this week—

I don't know. It all looks the same
from here: the ripening
of her breasts, the arduous yet deeply felt
Northern landscape, the pair of tweezers

I almost didn't remember.
Who knows? It could be I'm a wall
upon which someone's projecting a slide show,
some Mediterranean scenery, some

Jackson Pollocks, some slightly personal
bedroom antics (she's
undressing under the bed, he's
got a raw light bulb in his mouth

and a coat hanger wrapped around his legs.)
Oh, what happened to childhood?
Did it really, like a paper sailboat,
get hung on a rock or a twig?

Are you my mother? Hand me an iceberg
and I'll throw it through your window
or I'll worship inside it
as if it were a Gothic Cathedral

and I, a human being.
I don't know which is worse:
a fresh pot of coffee
or to be crossing a street late at night

somewhere in the West—Nebraska, say,
or Wyoming—anywhere there's a diner
open twenty-four hours, a man in a grey suit
hanging from a meat-hook.

Amnesia

I like that movie.
It reminds me of when I was six years old
and someone spilled vermouth
all over me at a gallery opening.

Or the time when, not so long ago,
I attempted to scale the Empire State Building
upside-down, and I broke the record
for "Unsuccessful Ideas Carried Out."

O it's a life. It is, in fact,
something I'd rather not think about
but have to, since it's black,
covers many, many miles and sounds

like a symphony by Shostakovich.
Have you ever seen the moon
dressed up like Greta Garbo?
I have! The world is too small

to get lost in. We need a few extra
hallways, a couple more doors
that open onto endless deserts—O
we need another napkin, thank you....

I was once an Indian Chief.
And then I stopped
calling everyone I knew by their last names
and started, instead, dying my hair green.

Those were the days.
But, when you've seen as many car wrecks as I have
you begin to imagine you're someone else
or a flower blooming on a hillside.

Or a love letter
edged in black, no return address,
no name, no lock of hair
glued to the upper right hand corner...

Amnesia

I see "Astronauts"
and I think "Laundry,
I have to do my laundry."
Or I think of a song

that goes "Every angel is terrible.
The sun rose
like a foot beneath the covers. Excuse me,
you have something on your upper lip,"

etcetera. It takes a whole year
to sing all the verses.
And then it rains some and the main character
gets shot. And then he dies.

Or rather,
and then he died.
I have no faith in chairs
or yawning smiles.

Only in the endless possibilities
of fallen leaves.
Just think of what you could do
with an entire mountain!

God, I'm getting a little excited.
I think maybe I should take a train
to northern Wisconsin.
I've heard that the people there actually seen to be snowing.

When they speak, you hear wind
instead of words.
When they make love,
icicles cling to their limbs.

Yes you too can learn to look at a mattress
as if it were a galaxy.
Just call by midnight tonight.
That number again…

Cowboys and Indians

She said can I help you I said
who is Clair de Lune and where
is the lost continent of Denison, Texas?
Can I have a slice of coconut pie?

Most things are pretty hard to understand.
Toilets, for instance. Or Beethoven.
I once got shot in the back
in a dream of my childhood. It was raining.

You know, there's not much difference between the moon
and a piece of paper. They both exist!
If your name is George or David, duck!
If your name is Stanley, please step up

to the reception desk—you have a phone call.
It's some woman—she says
I have seen you everywhere,
in the orchids, the Yellow pages,

the wrong side of the tracks, my eyes.
How have we come so far from Lubbock
and learned so little about love
and the nature of coffee and donuts,

the relation between wind and the bending branch.
You dreamed me
as you walked up the steps of the park
overlooking the white city, seeing me

in every distant pedestrian
and eucalyptus. I was air. My love,
something has happened to my eyes.
Listen—I'm dead.

Mollusks and Mankind

You make one move for that door
you're ancient history, you're Julius Caesar
in drag, walking the Tenderloin district
of San Francisco, where many wooden houses

make this city one of the most charming –
if you can't hear me, turn up the volume –
"supposed to meet me at the Fisherman's Wharf,
one of those bars supposed to seem like a ship:

ropes on the wall, brass railings,
flying fish" – hey, come back,
I'm getting to the important section
on human relations, it'll solve all your problems:

it will be like a hallway in a hospital
late at night, when the lobster shift
float like angels in the green light
so filled with occasional coughs and silence

who could ever doubt the existence of love?
Okay, time for a definition. Love:
1) a large, green and white sofa,
2) a person transfixed on an aquarium

in a dime store, 3) a word
which changes the color of someone's eyes,
4) a highway interchange (see "mufflers"),
5) the butt of a rifle, bashing someone's head in –

Whoops! didn't mean to get serious.
It's just that I love you, love you
autumnally, and look at all the leaves
and the patterns they make on the sidewalk after the rain

and look at my hand – it's shaking.
Why is my hand shaking? Why
are you not saying anything?
Are you at the bottom of a lake, smiling?

Soliloquy Beginning in Anger

Not only is the moon fucked, you're fucked, I'm
fucked, the el-train full of sleepers is fucked,
even that laundry hanging out to dry
between two tenements is fucked. It's all fucked!...

Jesus!...Glad I got that out of my system!
So here are some beautiful images. Enjoy:
Rows and rows of empty folding chairs
at dawn, around the bandshell, the whole world

covered with dew, at different times, of course,
a thin silk nightgown, taken off
and put back on, arms extended upwards
till the straps fall back in place and morning

puts its apron on and starts to work
painting everything a different color, the fragile
china, blue and white, the walls
a thick coat of raw umber, the ceramic

pitcher, a Milking-Maiden beige
till at last the sleeper's eyes unhinge
on a scene somewhat familiar: it's June
in a field of golden-rod, tall

and still as a couple of cowboys just before
a shoot-out, necks tensed, fingers extended,
elbows jutting into the past-tense of never, ready –
and now, the main event: a ton of fish

falling through the ceiling, knocking over
bar-stools and half-drunk mugs of beer,
Marshal Dillon
standing at the swinging doors,

pistol drawn:
"Miss Kitty?
Festus?
Doc?"

Whoopy Tie Yie Yoe

Amongst the phlox and burnt-orange lilies flaming
like noon on the pavement around the swimming pool,
the eucalyptus bowing their heads in beneficence
like monks, you used to say, amongst the ferns,

there comes your figure down the shaded sidewalk,
your mellifluous motions and white clogs
and silent hair long as the Brahms Sonata
for Clarinet and Piano in C# Minor

cascading around your waist—if you were a seashore
I'd lie on you every day, grey sky,
fog and tremendous winds withstanding, why
I'd fill my shoes with your sand, I'd

start collecting sea horses and eat linguini
with white clam sauce. That's one thing.
But why did you stop speaking to me?
Certainly you didn't think I'd

idealized you? No… I am not romantic.
I'm a Cubist (yucca yucca). I think
all I need to know is in your lips
and the way when, turning away from me, you smile

and I don't even know how I know you're smiling
and your shoulders are raised slightly, your white sweater
curving to the curve of your lovely back—
I place my hand on your cheek and we're immortal

as a postcard of the desert
minus all cacti, jackelope, cowboys, etc.
(I know that's difficult arithmetic)
leaving a sky as blue as your eyes, and a cloud.

Conversation With Inflatable Doll

That velvet painting of Elvis Presley
nailed above our vibrating bed kind of makes me feel
good and bad, if you know what I mean
and I think you do – gimme some bourbon – like

the purple jonquils' gossip of spring in the freezing rain –
talk is cheap and love is a graveyard
dragged along in a little red wagon
with one wheel missing – through the desert – ha ha –

hey let's you and me take a trip to the desert,
a honeymoon of herpes and tumbleweeds,
barbiturates and snapshots of cactus pears
and high-heeled shoes in the clouds –

just close your eyes and I'll be there
like the Morton Salt Girl's
white umbrella, sheltering nothing
an RC Cola and a razor wouldn't cure.

There's hardly anything that doesn't have to do with something else.
Take B-movies
and mental institutions for example
(everybody loves somebody sometimes).

Many people like to fist-fuck.
I just found this out recently.
You see, my world is like a gold-fish bowl
without any fish. Thus the lipstick.

And thus the fact that every time I try to kiss you,
an old waitress appears at the door of our room
bearing a tray with some after-dinner mints
and a pair of loaded revolvers.

Girl Accuses Father of Taping Her Mouth Shut

I never was any good at underwater Macbeth.
I always forgot my lines and said things like
I think our friendship is really important.
A large duck galloped across the horizon.

Many people spoke German.
I love you, and you are crushing my ribs
with your tractor. A man walks into a bar
and orders several German Shepherds to go.

I love a parade!
However, I think there's something funny about
the way you're always shoving a flashlight
down my throat. Do you think that's attractive?

The other day I was in Vegas and
an aubade for narcissus blooms and freight train
was performing in a cadmium field
to an audience of broken chairs

and suitcases and grapefruit rinds and shoes.
The world was a good idea.
It's just that
too many people left their phone off the hook.

I can't really think of any reason
to stop throwing this brick at the mirror—
In a room far away, a drawer is closed
and in the drawer is a leaf in a diary

of someone I've never even met
who's sitting in an arm-chair next to a fire—
writing these words to a former lover:
"When I think of your face, all I see is a closed post office."

December Mosaic

On the far left side is a couple embracing in a blizzard,
their legs submerged in the snow and faces lit
by a high intensity lamp in a window
of someone who's either drawing or writing a letter.

On the far right side, a huge bottle of vodka
with the word "God" inscribed on the black label.
Next to the bottle is a doghouse
which is issuing forth the word "dog."

How difficult a task it is, how difficult
a task to describe the whatnot which transpired.
Excuse me, my tea is boiling. I'll be back
in a minute – here, I'll turn on Handel's Messiah.

There now, where was I? Ah yes, the moon
shone like a Bach cantata over the universe
contained within the boundaries of the town
which contained many streets and houses and glazed hams.

All in the past tense, alas. Not
that the choir of angels doesn't still exist, but where?
When the angels stop singing, there are so many curtains,
and seashells on bathroom window sills.

There are so many crucifixes, evenings
of mortuary glances, lips snarling,
and novels open to pages with love scenes
that take place in Victorian bedrooms.

In the novel, there's always room for more
dime-store lingerie around the ankles,
diamond districts and men in black hats.
In the crucifix, there's only room for a word:

encyclopedia. That's it, too, pardner.
Just a desert of empty conversations,
fruitless insanities, and long, long tables
piled high with chicken bones and napkins.

Trip to the Salad Bar

Well let me ask you this:
When you open the iron gates to the forest
and the leaves are starting to fall and you hear
everywhere the sounds of typewriters

do you think of me, or the elevator
operator of the elevator
that takes one from the subway station
at 190th Street to the Cloisters:

a small fan is bolted to the corner
and a chair, like a Perry Mason re-run,
is occupied by a fat man
reading Spider Man comic books…?

You go to the all-night drugstore,
okay, and there are these telephone booths,
okay, in the back of the joint and these two gangsters,
okay, are like shooting each other through the glass, like

a summer's day, but not at all like
your oceanic tresses and your voice
which opens up the hyacinth
and irises after the rainstorm.

If I were an acorn or the speed of light,
you wouldn't treat me half as bad as you do.
Why do you treat me like a Dry-Cleaners
with potted ferns hanging in the window?

Why do Northern European painters
emphasize the suffering of Christ?
Why do you stare at me like I'm a word
and you're a park with benches and a fountain?

Would you like to have lunch some time?
Would you give me a reason to get off the floor?
Would you hand me that bottle of vodka, or at least
would you close all the curtains and hand me my monk's robe?

Romantic Love, 1987

It's best this way: you, a winding staircase
in a nineteenth-century monastery;
me, a pack of Lucky Strikes
wadded up, empty, purely decorative now.

But, hey—

IV

Ode to a Nightingale Revisited

My name is John and I'm an alcoholic.
My heart aches tonight because I've been thinking
about the time
That a drowsy numbness pained my sense. God. My worst
day sober
Is better than the feeling of drinking some dull opiate
to the drains.
In fact, I can honestly say that I have no desire
To be a bird. Well…certain days – ha ha ha ha –
But seriously, I'm happy just to be a thin, pale, sickly,
Slightly effeminate Englishman staying sober one day at
a time.

*

I have a disease. It makes me want a draught of vintage
That hath been cooled a long age in the deep-delved earth.
See – listen to me! I still crave it! Not one day
goes by
That I don't consider picking up a drink. It's not
through envy
Of thy happy lot, distant bird, but being too happy in
thine happiness
That thou, light-wingéd Dryad of the trees, are able to
drink socially –
What am I talking about? This is a bird! Birds don't drink!
Of course then the committee in my head starts saying
"Yes they do."

*

Thanks for letting me share.

Ode to the Brooklyn Zoo

I went to the Brooklyn Zoo to see the polar bear collection
and think about my personal problems, such as
Why am I still so alone when all my friends
are getting married and having babies.
The air felt just like mid-October in a Stuttgart
so far removed that no one's still around
to savor the memory of its heated streusels. The leaves, though,
were green as mid-July. Could it be
the smell of smoke that filters through the trees
of the park, or is that too just something
carried from another place that's vanished like a coffin
from Wisconsin, a lawn party everyone's left.
The polar bears look like they're having fun,
though they are lugubrious, incarcerated, and obviously
in the wrong climate. I have made many mistakes,
o pals o' mine, like moving to a cabin in the woods
to live among the moose and permafrost – and then,
as if that weren't bad enough, renouncing rustic monk-hood
to live amongst the crying babies and smiling teeth,
not to mention the subway platforms.
The pretzel vendors move their carts out in the dewy morning
then more or less stand in one place all day,
in front of the zoo or the library, selling pretzels
to random individuals. When the day is done,
or when there are no more pretzels to sell, they pack it up
and roll their carts back silently to obscure storage facilities
near water, enveloped in late-day shadows.
Pizza Boy is always walking in the same direction
with a great big Chef-Boy-R-Dee smile on his blank slate
of a face, a little too oblivious for my taste.
There are skirts being pulled up for crying out loud!
Or am I the only one who sees this?
My white and woolly wompatriots from the North can't even hear me,
still doped up as they are, probably, on those tranquilizer darts
used to subdue them into the chopti-copter's
special "Polar Bear Transport Unit" – just a big hammock, really,
attached to the flying machine vis-à-vis a system of ropes and pulleys,
rather flimsy, if you ask me, for such a task,
inadequate, irresponsible… even dangerous!
I want to love everyone. I really do.
If only Jesus Christ were here to help me,
I'd walk behind Him, dodging air-borne chairs and tables
thrown by a Man who hadn't had that crucial "second cup"
of coffee that would enable Him to love "all humanity."
That's reality. No one's nice all the time. But some people
seem to be able to put on a pretty good act
over Sauvignon Blanc and flickering candle light imbued

with an appropriately subtle scent: "Grandpa's Sock Drawer"
or "I Remember What Sex Is" –
the right degree of sincerity in the eyes, the proper amount
of determination in the voice, manly, yes,
but not afraid to eat a couple of pubic hairs
if that's what it takes to prove sensitivity, devotion
and Honor. I was such a man once.

*

One sees egrets, pelicans, Great Blue Herons,
hoards of pink flamingos, all of them pointing
in the same direction without a single thought among them
it would seem, ducks, of course, geese, swans, and a plethora
of nervous little shore-birds skinny-leggedly scurrying this way and that –
in other words, not very goal-oriented: one sees
such things, but not at the Brooklyn Zoo.
Here one sees red brick
and brown brick – i.e., buildings.
Inside the buildings, there are animals.
This much has been ascertained
by a variety of silent individuals.
The animals look scared.
One animal is most assuredly a giraffe,
though I have never seen his head.
The one who sits alone in the shadows
might be a gorilla – or it might not.
It's too big to be a chimpanzee,
and far too human to be a water buffalo.
Whatever it is, there have been noises on occasion
like that of a little girl crying.
One must shake one's head and move on. The lion cage
is always empty. It would appear
there isn't actually a lion.
And yet we stand and wait, all of us,
staring into the void, waiting for something
that has never appeared, though fresh feces
would suggest otherwise. One must,
again, move on. Hey there, Mr. Polar Bear!
(Now we're outside again, in the waning light of summer.)
Remember that news item several years back
about the 3 boys who climbed into the polar bear cage
at this very zoo? I remember it. There were 3 of them.
They climbed into the polar bear cage, or cave, rather,
and were promptly devoured by the polar bears.
The zoo was closed.
It was late at night.

No one heard their screams as the mighty, ferocious
and extremely bored polar bears ripped their little bodies to
shreds, leaving only 3 baseball caps, which, apparently,
the bears were wearing the very next morning,
sideways, you know, with attitude.
Yo – no justice, no peace.
They didn't ask to be wrenched from their home
and detained indefinitely in a cramped, hot space
only to be gawked at by idiots.
They didn't sign up for this shit know wha'm sayin'?

*

Words.

*

I just figured out what my biggest problem is:
I'm too self-analytical.
Or maybe (maybe?) I'm not self-analytical enough.
I don't know. Other problems include: moroseness,
cynicism, pessimism, lack of self-confidence
and laziness. Walking past the owl cage, I wonder
What am I doing here? At the zoo?
In the middle of a week-day?
I look around and all I see are Caribbean women
pushing rich white people's babies around in baby carriages
and I wonder What is the purpose of Art?
To instruct and delight, as Aristotle tells us repeatedly
in a thick Scottish brogue and false moustache?
Often I feel like Custer at the Battle of Little Big Horn
infused with a 1970s ultra-nostalgic sepia tone,
all warm and glowy en route to the Last Hurrah.
Hurrah. Apparently, it's not an uncommon emotion.
Everyone's losing at something.
It just matters more to some people, for example, Orpheus
or Ty Cobb. However, unlike baseball, Art
turns loss into triumph, a spinning-plate routine
performed by a man with a bad toupee
and pants that are both too short
and too tight. Just look at him go,
running back and forth like his life depended on those plates
continuing to spin. Course,
I 'fose his life do depend on it, the uhm watchemecallit – plates.
It's always what you can't see that kills you.

Ode on Complexity

The fact that you're a lesbian,
The fact that your imitation leopard-skin panties exist,
The fact that I exist in relation to your imitation leopard-skin panties,
Other facts:
The moon,
The ocean,
Dostoyevsky,
Came not Piero della Francesca by usura,
Subway tokens are a dollar,
I'm losing my mind,
The image of your body, again and again,
Will I ever see you naked again?
Will I ever write another decent poem?
Houses are built.
Apples keep falling from trees and conking people on the head,
Newspapers tell us of wars in third-world countries,
People firing machine guns at each other,
Harlequin romances tell us of registered nurses at midnight,
        taking off their stockings,
Encyclopedias tell us the history of Madagascar,
Jesus tells us to go into our closets and pray (Matthew B. IV, v. 3),
Existentialism vs. parking tickets,
Pro football players vs. the 13th century,
Should I take a shower tonight or wait till the morning?
Wittgenstein tells us that "each subject is a limitation
        of the world" but I wonder what he means by that—
Perhaps he means that in isolating a public restroom from
        the zoo in which it's located, one forgets entirely about
        the gorillas,
I keep thinking about you without any clothes on, or maybe wearing
        those black leotards,
I'm thinking Saint Cecilia has bowed her head and sunk into
        the shadows,
The harp strings are still and the angels retired to their painting,
Dunkin Donuts serves another creamless coffee and the night
        frost sparkles on the windshields,
Hounds bounding through the English countryside at dawn, bugles
        sounding, dried leaves crackling under foot and hoof,
Quarter moon appearing in the upper-right-hand corner of the page,
The fact that a building just exploded in Beirut,
The fact that your tongue inside my mouth is sounding
        like a good idea,
More than a good idea, the past,
The medieval tapestries hanging in museums,
The museum guard whose back is turned,
The way his spine fits together, piece by piece, covered up by skin,
The city, too, fits together after dark, traffic lights marking
        every vertebrae,

Men with knives lurk in darkened stairways and elevators, undone
zippers marking yet more pieces of the same decrepit back,
Not a constellation,
Not a line drawing by Matisse of a dove,
Not a naked woman
But a structure, a blueprint, a way of chalking lines around
dead human bodies, indelibly,
Not rain-soluble,
But an equation for understanding knife wounds and corporate
executives, 2 constants in a formula whose variable is women,
The fact that you're a lesbian, the fact that
Desire is a formula requiring absence,
Ground beef's a $1.59 a pound,
Italian fettuccine is expensive,
You are present in the snow-covered pine trees of northern Montana,
You continue to exist as my boardwalk's uprooted in a hurricane,
As coconuts fly through the dangerous air,
As people stand waiting to cross busy intersections in downtown
Minneapolis,
You are emptying an ashtray, bending over (I love to see you climbing
over things!),
Football players are taking off their clothes in the locker room,
Everyone is taking off their clothes!
No one is thinking of the parrot shrieking in the closed pet shop.
No one is thinking of the laundromat open 24 hours – the
change machine is broken –
No one is thinking of the plastic doll, whose lips are painted
in a smile abandoned in the graveyard of all places,
We must never stop singing in the choir of our private cathedral. Amen.
Glory be to pine trees, especially ponderosas, since they sort of
look like deciduous trees in their branch formation. The best
of both worlds
Oh lawd, lawd.
We must never stop sampling perfume bottles on the ground floors of major
department stores.
We must never stop holding hands.
Oh lord help us remember how sweet it is, when the leaves are
falling, or when the snow is falling, to hold each other's
hand.
And then there are the train stations.
Help us arrive on time when our love has traveled many miles
and help us remember to purchase some roses beforehand.
We must never stop exchanging small rocks as tokens of larger
things such as the Milky Way.
Black dogs are important.
We must never stop petting black dogs. Amen.
Gather ye rosebuds – huh uh.
You can pick up fossils, but don't keep them – that's against
the law. Amen.
Pick-up trucks are essential to getting around in the country.

Ode: Kritique of Pure Reason

If you look at a map of the universe
And compare it to an autumn day in New York City
You'll have to get past the basic structural differences
Such as: cigar shops, people walking their dogs through public parks,
    leaves always falling vs.
Indigo and limitless space encased inside a 2-dimensional rectangle
    3 by 5 feet, approximately—
Now, pretend you're the mad scientist who, with little attention to
    physical appearance or newspapers,
Must determine the velocity of a single electron in a vacuum which
    doesn't yet exist.
It's midnight: your laboratory is boiling over with various liquids
    you've long since forgotten about,
You're making no progress, years and years of work in vain, shelves of
    ledgers
Filled with essentially meaningless figures and information, and then—
    Ker-sploosh!—
How easy! There it is, like a mistress, undressing, shimmering,
    the moonlight so beautiful, the curtains blown open
By a sudden gust of— The Answer: If you want to understand an electron
You must become an electron, you must enter the world, the world
Your vacuum, its subways, and donut shops, its old men pissing on the
    glass partitions of enclosed bus-stop areas,
Under the moon, the same moon that shone through the windows of your
    limitless chamber
Overlooking the backs of apartment buildings in, as it were, a not-so-good
    neighborhood
Where, as welcome gestures, neighbors with unseemly scars around their
    eyes and mouths
Hit you up for whatever they think you can afford, then give you a little
    scar for fun
As if this were some adult form of tag – You're it! –
As if the scar were a torch and the person inflicting it a long distance
    runner
Come from Antiquity – O how many nights and odd turns, how many closed
    inns,
Cheap motel rooms buzzing with regional insects, large flying cockroaches,
    silver fish,
Inside the bathtub, trying to get out as you try to wash them down the
    drain,
Must also be a part of your experiment, that has so many variables now,
All you want are constants, so you turn to the Venus de Milo, her
    image
Spotlit against the tempestuous North Atlantic night: maybe she'll
    direct you towards the everlasting—
But no, she can't point too well these days, though she is very beautiful,
    white, unchanging,
Better than Marlene Dietrich even, in "The Blue Angel," statuesquely straddling
    a hard-backed chair,

Her fishnet stockings attracting much attention in the smoke-filled tavern—
but how camp really!—
How un-universal— how unlike Poussin, whose classical landscapes
you finally must – ahh… –
Defer to, if you want a Sense of Beauty: hush, we mustn't disturb that
gentleman there in the tweed coat
Deep inside a meditative rapture in front of Poussin's great "Rape of
the Sabine Women":
Such eternal balance, I mean in the arrangement of those flailing limbs,
how unified
The terror in the women's faces, and then the contrast of the women's
whiteness
Against the men's redness, not to mention those great big Roman columns
Without which this whole little world would just fall apart, I mean
the structure—
Hmmmmnnn…maybe architecture is the Way to go, the mother whose arms you
may go crying into,
And there's that special lasagna you love with spinach and ricotta,
steaming on the kitchen table,
How good it is to be home, where there's always a couple a milk cartons,
so you don't feel too bad
Pouring yourself a full glass whenever you're thirsty, and look, it's
snowing tonight, have to build a fire,
And then later, when everyone's gone to bed, think about architecture
a little, about fire-places,
About how fire-places used to be the central motif in many a Renaissance
poem
Symbolizing, archetypically, as you might imagine, women. Women and
architecture,
Like moonlight on the water, go together, are interchangeable, intertwined,
Like strands in a braid, Cynthia, Diosa del Mar, sprinkling stars across
the ocean
As she glides across the waves towards the viewer who carries her picture
in his wallet
For good luck, not necessarily luck with women so much as with ideals of
harmony
Which leads back to architecture, columns, moonlight, a bunch of grapes
Held above the lips of a man reclining in the ruins of the Parthenon,
A woman's fingers lowering them delicately into his mouth
As a rose-scented breeze blows through their tunics, and then:
Wa-OOO-ga! Mr. Architecture appears, feeling a little neglected, calling the
lovers' attention to the abstract
Beauty of their surroundings: Just look at that view of the moonlit
Aegean, look how well those columns are spread,
Look at that! a perfect view of the olive tree, its branches drooping down
in front of the distant torches
Illuminating Athens, city of departures, city of women with flaming eyes
Burning little crosses in the hearts of the boys sprouting flowers out of
their mouths
Instead of words, would they could cry the words "enthroned dagger!"

V

Sestina: My Women

I am in love with 6 women: Indra,
who is not speaking to me; Colleen,
who has not returned any of my letters; Suzy,
who says I need to learn how to look "happier"; Liz,
who lives in New York and only dates tall men; Jenny,
about whom I know nothing; and Atsuko,

a beautiful Japanese woman with whom I sense no chemistry. Atsuko
speaks to me but never returns my phone-calls. Indra,
on the other hand, has not even given me her new number. Jenny
hasn't given me her number either, but I haven't asked. I think Colleen
is really the girl for me – so intimate, sweet, and beautiful. But it's Liz
who really turns me on, sexually, I mean. I find Suzy

attractive too, though she is abrasive, manipulative, and attached. Suzy
looks me straight in the eyes when she talks, and puts her hand on my knee,
unlike Atsuko
who retains a cool distance. Well, that's not true. Last time… Hmm. I wish Liz
would put her hand on my knee, but she lives 3,000 MILES AWAY, as does Indra
with whom I was engaged, 2 times, briefly. With Colleen
there has been no physical contact. Same with Jenny.

Of course I've only exchanged 20-25 words with Jenny.
But they've all been quality words. She's a baker. Suzy
bakes, too. She wants to open a restaurant with toasters on each table. Colleen
lives on a farm in Kentucky. She'll probably never leave. Atsuko,
like me, has lived everywhere: New York, Virginia, The Philippines. Indra
is scared to leave her apartment, or her bed, for that matter. She knows Liz

but can't stand her – Liz is a Republican. I like Liz
because of her butt – Oooops! I meant to say, uhm… Jenny
is the only person who really acts nice towards me. That counts. Indra
was a jerk. Her last words to me? "What you need is a mental health care
professional." Suzy,
I'm sure, would be even worse. Good thing she's unavailable. About Atsuko
I've heard some real horror stories. (Doctor Jekyl & Mrs. Hyde) And poor Colleen,

so sweet, so young, has herself been the unfortunate recipient of jerky
behavior. Colleen
was screwed over by an up-and-coming Country & Western star. That would
never happen to Liz,
who is always in control, and who, besides, only dates lawyers.
That's interesting. Atsuko,
too, has dated a lot of lawyers. I wonder why? Stability? Hmmm…
I don't think Jenny
would ever go out with a lawyer. But hey – I don't know her. Suzy
lives with a bartender. They might be married. I was to marry Indra,

but Indra was too young for me: 25. Yes. That's the reason. And Colleen
is only 22. Suzy's about 27, I'd say. And Liz
is one year younger than me: 29. Jenny's…25, maybe? 31 is the age of Atsuko.

Sestina: Elk vs. Non-Elk

Recently, I divided the world into 2 columns: "elk"
and "non-elk." Under "non-elk," I wrote "Bill,"
"underwear," "France," Duke Ellington's song "Take the A Train,"
personal home computer systems, which I do not advise you to utilize,
especially when you're sitting in your reclining chair, or "barcalounger,"
trying to think of a word

that might fit in the "non-elk" column, which contains every word
except, of course, for "elk."
"Silly?" you say, reclining in your favorite barcalounger,
channel-surfing, bored stiff, as if your name were "Bill"
or "Bob" or even "Chet," a name that one might utilize
to describe my Uncle Chet, who has the personality of a train.

That's not true. Any train,
it must be said, has more to say than Uncle Chet, whose only spoken word,
mumbled from the back-seat of a car, sometimes, is "utilize."
I'm not lying. One evening Chet was watching TV when an elk
burst through the wall. Impaled on one antler was a bill
for 20,000 bagels. Did Chet budge an inch from his barcalounger?

Chet did not, and not a word was spoken, except by the barcalounger
who – Wait a minute. What happened to my train
of thought? O where did it get derailed? Conductor Bill,
where are we? Nebraska? North Dakota? I'd like a word
with the driver, please. Why aren't we moving? Elk
must have something to do with this inertia here, home on the range, where "utilize"

is a word seldom heard – in fact, it's discouraged. Were you to utilize
the word "utilize," you might find yourself strapped to a barcalounger,
catapulted over the prairie, only to land on the unsuspecting antlers of an elk
whose unwitting impalement would surely unhinge the unlucky passengers on this lame train
that has arrived, one diphthong short of a Welsh word,
in Nowheresville, the home of my very dear Aunt Bill.

And now I feel exactly like a duck bill
quack quack quacking foolish garbage, attempting to utilize
a certain metaphoric logic, that I may recall the one word
capable of making me lurch from my barcalounger
(of despair) and into the air (of reason) where I need not train
my thoughts on anything besides the concept… "elk"!

An elk named Bill
explored his motivation as a character. The train's aim was to utilize
Man's Inhumanity to Barcalounger. Uhm, word.

Sestina: A Cowboy's Diary

May 14: Another miserable night. Rain
fell. Wind blew. Was on my horse the whole night.
Cattle left us. Not one beefe
to be seen. May 15: Hunt beeves
is the word. May 16: 195 beeves
recovered 14 miles from camp. Beeves

well near starved. May 18th: Indians came & tried to take our beeves.
Would not let them. May 19th: Scarfed jerky in rain.
May 22: Wind & rain & lightning: 200 beeves
got away. Was on my horse the whole night.
May 23rd: had to cross a river with beeves.
Was attacked by a beefe.

May 24th: Was attacked by another beefe!
May 27th: Dad-blamed beeves!
Stampede last night. Lost 2 men. Beeves
ungovernable. Rain
heavy at times. Can't recall a more miserable night.
May 30th: Beeves

ran, in the a.m. In the p.m., attended lecture on beeves
at local university. Very interesting. Found out that a beefe
will not defend his self against a beefe. That night,
hunt whores was the word. Found beeves
instead – 100 of them. Another stampede in the rain.
Next morning we found more beeves.

June 1st: I thought I saw some beeves
but was mistaken. Went into town for counseling. Beeves
occupied my thoughts. When I close my eyes, I see rain
and that same strange image again and again: a beefe
with the body of a man is yodeling to the other beeves
who somehow turn into ladies of the night.

June 2nd: This cognitive approach seems to be working. Last night,
only had one bad dream about beeves.
Therapist says: Lay off the beeves.
Gave me a great book called "Men Who Love Beeves
Too Much." Very insightful. It makes a good point about how a beefe
don't care about me, and yet I give and give. June 3rd: Rain.

June 4th: More rain. June 5th: Hard night.
June 9th: Found one stray beefe. Then lost 3 beeves.
June 10th: Found beeves. June 12th: Lost beeves...

1-800-VOCABULary

USE MORE WORDS!
For a low monthly charge, you can increase your vocabulary
by *600* words. Yes, *600 words*! To wit: "Costermonger":
a hawker of fruits, vegetables, fish, etc.; "Pulchritudinous":
physically beautiful, comely; "Anthroposophy":
a spiritual and mystical philosophy based on the teachings of Rudolph Steiner.

It is not so crucial to actually know anything about Rudolph Steiner
himself so much as it is to KNOW MORE WORDS
like – wait, where'd I put it – "anthroposophy."
Yes, you can actually feel your vocabulary
expanding as those brain cells increase to allow more space for "pulchritudinous,"
uhm, "costermonger."

You're at an important banquet. "Costermonger"
suddenly occurs to you during a lull. You blurt it out, and Rudolph Steiner,
of all people, appears out of nowhere, to congratulate you on your "pulchritudinous"
understanding of WORDS.
"What a vocabulary!"
he crows, NOT knowing YOU know HE invented ANTHROPOSOPHY.

"WELL," you say, winking at the invisible studio audience, "How's your
ANTHROPOSOPHY
going these days? COSTERMONGER! COSTERMONGER!
COSTERMONGER!"
Vocabulary
is key. It has to do with Rudolph Steiner
and how he and others like him respond to YOU. Words
are what make you *pulchritudinous*.

Take the word "pulchritudinous,"
for example. Or "anthroposophy."
By now, you should be able to use these words
comfortably in most social situations. Repeat after me: "costermonger."
That's right! You've got it! You don't have to be Rudolph Steiner
to show off your new and very impressive vocabulary.

For years, I labored at cocktail parties with little or no vocabulary,
using hand signals and facial expressions to communicate words like
"pulchritudinous."
I'm not stupid, nor are you. But neither one of us is Rudolph Steiner.
Again, you DON'T have to be the inventor of ANTHROPOSOPHY
to slyly insert "COSTERMONGER"
into a discussion of Italian-American immigration. Words

are how we talk. "Words" is the same thing as "vocabulary,"
basically? Though a "costermonger" is usually not described as "pulchritudinous,"
"anthroposophy" *was* invented by "Rudolph Steiner"!

Sestina: Bob

According to her housemate, she is out with Bob
tonight, and when she's out with Bob
you never know *when* she'll get in. Bob
is an English professor. Bob
used to be in a motorcycle gang, or something, or maybe Bob
rides a motorcycle now. How radical of you, Bob –

I wish I could ride a motorcycle, Bob,
and also talk about Chaucer intelligently. Bob
is very tall, bearded, reserved. I saw Bob
at a poetry reading last week – he had such a Bob-
like poise – so quintessentially Bob!
The leather jacket, the granny glasses, the beard – Bob!

and you were with my ex-girlfriend, Bob!
And you're a professor, and I'm nobody, Bob,
nobody, just a flower-deliverer, Bob,
and a skinny one at that, Bob –
and you are a large person, and I am small, Bob,
and I hate my legs, Bob,

but why am I talking to you as if you were here, Bob?
I'll try to be more objective. Bob
is probably a nice guy. Or that's what one hears. Bob
is not, however, the most passionate person named Bob
you'll ever meet. Quiet, polite, succinct, Bob
opens doors for people, is reticent in grocery stores. Bob

does not talk about himself excessively to girlfriends. Bob
does not have a drinking problem. Bob
does not worry about his body, even though he's a little heavy. Bob
has never been in therapy. Bob,
also, though, does not have tenure – ha ha ha – AND Bob
cannot cook as well as I can. Bob

never even heard of paélla, and if he had, Bob
would not have changed his facial expression at all. Bob
is just so boring, and what I can't understand, Bob –
yes I'm talking to you again, is why you, Bob,
could be more desirable than me. Granted, Bob,
you're more stable, you're older, more mature *maybe* but Bob…

(Months later, on the Bob-front: My former girlfriend finally married Bob.
Of Bob, she says, "No one has taken me higher or lower than Bob."
Me? On a dark and stormy sea of Bob-thoughts, desperately, I bob.)

VI

Description of the Universe

Telephone's ringing. Mesquite trees are howling
in the desert wind. I give my hand to you.
Lizards stare into the western sky.

* * *

An acolyte is someone who kneels before a backdrop
of grey clouds. During eternity, answers fall in a
shower of beautiful, white monosyllables. What's
funny are the particulars: Christ's blue eyes, the
fact that Alaska is cold, and that I desire you, whose
back is turned like a season or a forest I remember.
Ah, the melancholy of ecstasy, the orange sky
lingering over the train station.

* * *

Already, the harbor is moored this evening. Those ships
retain the moods of the places they've docked in:
Hawaii, Vladivostok, Guam, undoubtedly. I am afraid
to tell you certain things. So, instead, I will crawl into
the jaws of Leviathan. And I won't come out…

* * *

I hand you a newspaper. Years later, you forget. The stars
are the same, almost. A recording of Malagueña plays
inside my soul. There's a staircase. Someone lights a
match. It burns out (I'm an atheist). I'm a summer in
Honolulu – and you can't be there. The waiter hands
you your piña colada, which you hold above your head
like the torch of the Statue of Liberty. There are waves.

* * *

There are thousands of doves, and all of them are stuffed,
on display, or simply depicted crudely on panels behind
the stuffed ones that are glued to the floor which is a
green field in North America. (Probably the Midwest.)
Observe their patience, how calm they are, standing
there, on the eve of their migration to the Gulf. Their
cooing is unbearable.

* * *

Now here's something you might be interested in: a little
knickknack I picked up in China, years ago, before the
apocalypse. You can see for yourself, of course, that
it's the mood on the edge of a once-great city, Sunday
morning. Don't believe me? Well here's an entrance –
apréz vous – beneath the frieze of the fighting lovers.
You just follow that hallway and soon you'll have at
your disposal, everything that exists, or ever did exist,
all within the walls of the famous invisible rooms.

* * *

Keep an eye on the lion. And send me a postcard. Say:
"The rain falls down like a familiar thigh." I love you,
you whose eyes are as "cold and passionate as the dawn."
But I'm the protagonist, the one with the Spanish hat and
the whip. My cousin, the rockcrusher, says hello (in his
sleep). I would like, before I set down my cloak and pistol
for the night, to see you peel an orange once more.

Amnesia

I have no idea what I was going to say.
Something to do with traveling to Africa, maybe…(?)
I have no idea what I was going to say.
Well, actually, here's one image

I had wanted to put in this poem…uhh…
Well, actually, here's one image
that just sort of came to me one day:
in some forest, somewhere, a young girl.

That just sort of came to me one day.
Some call it inspiration – I call it genius.
A young girl, all by herself, laughing.
Some call it inspiration – I call it genius:

a young girl, all by herself, laughing,
just laughing! For no reason!
She's in the middle of the Black Forest
just laughing! For no reason!

She's in the middle of the Black Forest.
There are no other human beings
and it's two o'clock in the afternoon.
There are no other human beings.

And, it's two o'clock in the afternoon.
Okay, now that I've established the time and place
perhaps a little background info might be…
Okay, now that I've established the time and place

perhaps a little background info might be…
helpful…no…interesting…no…necessary…
Yes! Yes! That's it! It might be –
helpful?…no…interesting?…no…necessary!

Yes! Yes! That's it! It might be
necessary, i.e., a Caribbean moon
rose over the Café Espéjo.
"Necessary": i.e., a Caribbean moon

rose over the Café Espéjo –
that's Spanish for "mirror" – the young girl
walked and walked through the Forest of Dreams –
that's Spanish for "mirror" – the young girl

walked and walked through the Forest of Dreams
laughing hysterically, her little jaws

opening and closing, almost mechanically – she was
laughing hysterically, her little jaws

opening and closing, almost mechanically – she was
not, as it were, "alive."
It's not because of some sort of Frankenstein/Dracula character that she was
not, as it were, "alive."

It's not because of some sort of Frankenstein/Dracula character that she was,
to put it bluntly, dead.
No, she wasn't dead – it was her flesh that was
to put it bluntly, dead.

No, *she* wasn't dead – it was her flesh that was
green and covered with black sores.
Her eyes were like two gusts of wind, but her flesh was
green and covered with black sores.

Her eyes were like two gusts of wind, but her flesh was…
I have no idea what I was going to say.
Something to do with traveling to Africa, maybe…(?)
I have no idea what I was going to say.

Hair Club for Corpses

Before

Here's an example of what I used to be like:
miles and miles of steel mills, shut down,
snowed in, as viewed from a bridge
that takes you into the grey hills
on the edge of town,
at day's end, year's end,
where no one has a face.

After

And here's what I'm like now:
a long wooden table
in the dining hall of a medieval castle
where only the light of torches
illuminates a dinner of suckling pig
at a party in which all guests
are conspicuously absent,
leaving the host in an awkward position
of suspended animation,
his primitive knife and fork held upright,
his sackcloth napkin tucked into his fur-covered garment,
his Viking helmet
a little too big for his head.

The Orchid Shop

The year was 1962.
The place – Dallas, Texas.
The restaurant was underwater.
The trout were speaking German.

It was unclear as to why
we had all been strapped to our chairs.
The moon was a stranger on the edge of town.
And no one speaks to strangers.

Except for prostitutes
and switchboard operators. Baby –
you don't want to know
about the dogs with rat-masks attached to their faces.

You don't want to know about Vermeer.
He was a seventeenth-century Dutch painter.
Baroque. Invented the "camera obscura."
Some people call him the first "photo-realist."

Sorry. Anyway, the rest is really hard to piece together:
The conductor was naked.
Genevieve had disappeared.
The doorways were coffins. Who was Alfonzo?

The rain machine
had been turned on inadvertently.
Several couples were dancing
cheek to cheek, in the darkened store display.

And all that night, as we were making love
on the floor beneath the dress-rack,
I saw between the legs of the mannequins:
two lips, pressed against the glass.

Soliloquy on Botticelli Ave

Her lips were alizarin crimson and her eyes,
eyes were like a train station: empty,
full of storage lockers, pale green
and from her wrists, sunsets fell forever
like cigarettes extinguished in restaurant ashtrays,
like highways seldom traveled, her nineteenth century
hair was the same as drinking Pinot Noir
on invisible verandas, with Beethoven's
Pastoral Symphony turned up so loud
no conversation was possible—hands,
her hands, how can I describe her hands…
her hands were like the ocean, full of fish
and seaweed, her neck, si je m'en souviens,
her neck was as long as July—it made me sweat
and there were honeysuckle blossoms and fireflies
and in the evenings, people sat on porches
and said nothing—and occasional rainstorms
let loose from her entire body, and the leaves,
the leaves were still afterwards and dripping
for hours and her back was like a trellis
of wisteria—there was a fountain
implied in her smile, a garden no one walked in
but saw all the moonflowers bloom in the midnight
of her voice: "…pour moi, tu parles sans toucher,
sans parler—tu es une—" she's sleeping now—
hush—her legs are like a palace in winter,
the doors open, snow blowing in…

Season's Greetings from the Winter Family!

Well, another year has passed!
And, while it hasn't been a perfect one,
we have survived. Oh, first there was
the house burning down – everything ruined:
furniture, original artworks, priceless family heirlooms lost
because of some sort of electrical short
according to the arson squad
who, incidentally, interrogated us for 3 months,
making damaging allegations to our insurance company,
causing them to cancel our policy
before, alas, we could collect.
During that difficult period, Edith and I
both lost our jobs – just another case of
"corporate downsizing," I guess!
Fortunately, we did get a couple of rather
hefty severance packages which, unfortunately,
had to go almost entirely towards a deposit
on our new 2-bedroom apartment. You see, the landlord
asked that we pay 14 months in advance,
seeing as how we were both out of work
and had 3 kids to feed.
Two of our gang, Jason and Rebecca, I'm sad to say,
were taken away from us
by the Department of Human Services.
They said we were, quote,
"unable to provide a stable home environment or
adequate health-care"
(our health insurance was cancelled too).
Jason, as many of you know,
has acute agoraphobia – fear of open spaces,
fear of the world, basically –
and so he hasn't been outside
of his foster home for 4 months.
He receives his food through a slot
in his bedroom door.
The little guy only comes out late at night
to bathe and use the toilet.
We've discussed this problem with Jan and Bob,
his foster parents, and they've come to the conclusion
that Jason will change when he's ready.
In the mean time, his 18th birthday
is coming right up, and we're planning a BIG party
to which all of you are invited!
It promises to be a gala event!
Hopefully, Rebecca will be out of rehab
by then. She just turned 15
and, as fate would have it,

fell in with the wrong crowd.
When we saw her turning tricks
on Harry Hines, we knew it was
time to have a heart-to-heart.
We found out that our little Rebecca
has developed a bit of a drug habit – heroin –
and felt she had to turn to prostitution
in order to pay for it. Her pimp,
Mickey, threatened to kill all of us
for taking her away from him.
We offered to pay Mickey recompense
for his financial loss, and he responded
by stealing our car
and driving it off a cliff.
Because we also lost our car insurance,
Mickey's estranged wife, a transsexual
named Jill St. Jacques, is suing us
for every last penny, because, she says, legally
we are responsible for Mickey's death.
We can't afford a lawyer,
and so we do face a high possibility
of life imprisonment.
And, we have no way to get to our new jobs
out in the country,
on the chicken farm.
So, we've had to tighten the old belt
a few notches, dining nightly on cat food
and uncooked potatoes (all our utilities
have been shut off).
The adjustment to such a life has not been easy,
especially since our various medications ran out –
my high blood pressure pills, and Edith's,
well, valium!
Frankly, we've been a mess.
I'm afraid it hasn't been much of a cake-walk
for poor Barney, our youngest.
He's developed a whole range of obsessive-compulsive ticks
as a coping mechanism, we think.
Right now, as I type this,
little Barney is bouncing his head
against the floor – in multiples of three.
What usually happens now is our downstairs neighbors
crank their stereo really loud
until about 3 or 4 in the morning.
That's okay, though – we're being evicted
and must vacate by noon tomorrow.
So, don't bother sending any Christmas cards
this year. But do
have a very merry Christmas!

VII

Description of the Universe

The elk's expression is not so much one of fear
as of a stultifying bewilderment, an inability to discern
its relation to the fast-approaching object on the road
or what we humans call "the road," as we drive straight up
to the tundra. To carom off the sheer snowy drop-off
of a 13,000-foot mountain –
Well, yes: that's always a possibility.
But my traveling companion says that death must be
"the ultimate rush." All I see,
or can see from here beneath these banana trees,
sipping my piña colada, is the Universal Neighbor, removing groceries
from his luxury automobile, bemoaning the fact that he forgot to buy
green beans.
The waves don't care. They just keep on foaming on the white, white sand
and returning to nothing, the aquamarine and deep-blue passion
we call "the ocean." At the bottom,
the prehistoric fish are busy keeping the past intact
so we up here may live life to its fullest.
And yet, to exist without memory,
to live in a present untempered by the woodburning stove of the past,
is equivalent to trying to brew a cup of coffee without any water,
or Mrs. Langstrom's famous "soleless" shoe.
Memory is like a cargo ship.
And the cargo we unload contains not only such staples
as rice, grain, baby food, and, more likely than not, VCRs,
but as well the intangible, the tangerines
of our voluptuousity, the nectar we squeeze
above the full-bodied sensuous lips of our loved ones.
Desire returns again and again like the Avon Lady,
bearing a suitcase full of lipsticks and perfumes.
However,
the moment Marlene Dietrich appears in the fog
is the moment I'm out of here.
You can keep those champagne glasses –
I'm Memphis-bound, boys.

*

Those chickens are unnaturally large.
I realize that perhaps all chickens
would grow that large – if only they were allowed to live.
But how does that little rooster feel?
Not great, I bet.
I've wanted to tell you how I feel,
but the timing's always off –
either there's a room full of men playing guitars

or else we're in the cockpit of your brother's airplane
where conversation isn't possible.
Unless of course you turn off the engine.
And Richard Wanchisn – poor Richard Wanchisn.
He had provided something to talk about, though.
Sure we can talk about the stars:
That's the Big Dipper.
Or wait, maybe that's the Big Dipper.
Or how about farmlife in general:
Boy that drought has really done a number on the hay crop.
I hear that cattle sleep standing up.
If only we could see the hay-bales stacked
in the fields near twilight,
the way a horse will stand by a fence
wagging its tail…

*

How does one make sense of something that doesn't make sense?
New York, for instance.
That store on the corner that doesn't sell green olives.
Now what does that have to do with
Monet's Waterlilies?
And what about us
living in a world of leaky radiators
and dogs that don't like to be bathed?
Here,
the answers are far more important than the questions.
If you don't believe it, just try
giving a waitress the old silent treatment.

*

And still, the iceberg remains.
Our ship, jettisoned from safe passage through the Bering Strait,
awaits the doom that doom has planned.
The Arctic sun comes up for just an hour:
The dark sky lightens.
Each one of us is saying our prayers,
fingering our rosaries. Cap'm says
nor'easter's on its way.
We'll just have to wait it out
as rations dwindle, and ice floes crack and heave.
Our ship is but a hunk of metal
bound for the black night of the next world…

*

I was under the impression
that a woman at the beach
had taken off her shirt
and was swinging her breasts around
freely in the breezes of twilight.
Her friends were laughing and the waves were cascading at their feet.
She stood with her hands on her hips
and arched her back so that her nipples pointed heavenwards.
Heavenly, I thought. This is as it should be.
The sky is blue. The sky is yellow too.
But, but –
why not take off those pants?
If you're going to write an opera,
you sure as heck should write the last act.
It's not fair to those singers,
standing around in old-style ascots and petticoats,
ready to gesture dramatically at any given moment.
That's devotion, friend.

*

Then someone fell off a cliff.
Yes, you feel responsible –
but how could you have known?
And had you known, what could you have done?
It was his choice to climb that craggy peak.
And besides, there were so many other things to see,
literally thousands of pine trees, hundreds of thousands,
extending into the blurry and mountainous distance,
and let's not forget the industrious mole
for whom the entire Frank Church River of No Return Primitive Wilderness Area
is but a single mole hill
on a muddy slope.
You saw an elk, as well.
But that was on another trip, long ago,
in a different part of the state.
You spent the night in a little log cabin
with Diana, Goddess of the Hunt,
who made love with you in a hot spring
and afterwards, the pine trees
still continued to smell like pine trees.

That night, with only the light from a wood-burning stove
to cast your shadows on the wall,
you stayed awake debating Truth vs. Beauty.
If you remember,
you were for Beauty.

*

Flush goes the toilet –
just as the impresario has ended his aria,
the fallen leaves behind him already being swept away
by stagehands.
Here we are, in this life, listening to the answering machine
and shaking our heads.
There are too many messages,
and none of them, alas, is what we wanted to hear.
And yet as we stroll along the pretty, wooded path
through the quaint New England of old age some day
we might just stop and sit on a rock
overlooking yellow mountains, and think, "Who has loved me
so much as to become invisible, rising like smoke
from an unseen chimney, challenging the world of darkness
to a duel?"

*

Gentle Reader: The question of how to speak
should never arise: You and I should be walking through the woods
in an autumn long since passed, perhaps documented
by a black & white photograph of you
in your familiar old raincoat,
turning away, staring out towards the pasture
where a few lonely hay-bales await to be hauled
by a truck full of farmhands from another century.
Is it possible to speak of an orange
without ever saying its name?
Our conversations in the dark
linger on through the summer
like –

*

(This is the point on the bus
where the fat lady gets up and sings
Mona Lisa. Lipstick is smeared around her mouth
which sparkles with gold.
In the rearview mirror, the eyes of the busdriver
watch intently, revealing neither fear nor approval.
The other passengers sleep
or stare out the window at the rain
which never stops. All over the city,
umbrellas are abandoned in garbage cans.
Cardboard boxes used for shelter
sag where the rain has pooled,
their residents long since fled for the subway.)

*

I seem to have forgotten everything.
Every Christmas I take the B-train out to Bay Ridge
and pick up a bucket of lingenberries
and maybe some prins-korv and vortlimpa, if they have it.
And every year I go to a different coffee shop
for a cup of hot chocolate.
Well, there are some things.
And the shadows.

All I wanted was someone to say my name.
I wanted to know I was alive
by the look in some girl's eyes as she handed me my change,
by the way someone might have kissed me before sleep,
by the way I might have noticed a curtain blown open
by an autumn wind,
by the way I might have waited for a bus several hours,
dodging in and out of the hot dog stand for warmth
as the temperature dropped to the teens.
All I wanted was someone to think about me
as she was walking to work, to adore me
in images of cloistered courtyards
and yellow leaves, to see me everywhere,
to crave
the touch of my hand in a Greyhound bus,
to fall asleep in my lap, to smile.
And then, when the snow was falling,
to walk home with me from the subway station.
I wanted to paint a mural that would cover the whole world,
that would save us from oblivion while also containing
miles and miles of telephone poles
and 2-lane highways no one travels.
I wanted to speak with the tongue of the lizard
and lips of the wolf and still
be taken seriously.
I wanted no less than to hop a box-car at 3 a.m. while also
undressing someone in my air-conditioned 1-bedroom apartment.

*

Ahhh…the Queen Wilhelmenna Tulip Garden at sunset…
Thus the windmill.
But where is the trout?
Where is that which we must perennially remind ourselves is necessary
for the proper viscosity breakdown, that Ideal Motor Oil
of the soul, which must be changed every several thousand miles,
the ideas we put in our heads while eating oranges,
the routes we take through the Prehistoric Fern Garden
(where one of the Ferns is raining, perpetually),

the languages we dream in,
the rowboat we paddle down the River Styx
and that black robe we all must wear when we arrive.
The moon never sets.
The wolf sees all from the edge of the forest,
our little light in the window we keep on
to scare off evil spirits, and guide us
as we wash the dishes or just
stare out at the night and our reflection,
more frightening than reassuring, but then we never were
an oasis, were we.
The "child inside us" has grown
and devours everything in sight like a Cyclops
on the loose without the distinction of ever having met Odysseus.
You think this is bad, wait'll you get that phone call
in the middle of the night, that thunderstorm
instead of a voice: You will turn to stone
and centuries later tourists will walk through your home
seeing you as only an example, a metaphor,
not that that's not valid, but is it the whole story.
Even the filmstrip of your childhood is incomplete.
They left out the jar full of praying mantises.
How many hours you stared at them as they groped
over each other's sticklike limbs, looking for a way out.
They didn't suffocate.
They just gave up.

*

What happened happened for no reason:
As if in a trance, the world
followed us everywhere, providing
the perfect background scenery: the moon,
as if on cue, rising behind Central Park,
and from your roof, even the lights of New Jersey
seemed romantic. Ah, focaccia...

What happens happens only once
and then is shelved away for eternity
in an extremely private library
with high ceilings and grates around the windows
on 86th (I think) between Park and Lex.
You pick up a yellow leaf –
10 years later it falls from a book: That's
how memory works. You're never prepared
for that black & white image of the Hotel Paris,
the elevator ride and the woman
who moans and sobs so much

that strings of snot pour from her face
in a crazy web to her hands
as you hold on tight
to the huge white hand of your father
who is tall as the Chrysler Building, and just as strong.
The existentialists are wrong:
The present is boring: just so much laundry detergent
poured or dumped into the washing machine
of despair.
God I love poetry.
Sure there's a mattress squeaking above your head.
Sure the universe is a murky place.
Sure – the aquarium smells bad – Yes! It's all true!
But I've got a one-way ticket to an unheard-of place.
Granny Winter's there, with her apron on,
frying up some chicken. Outside the screen door
are all the Novembers I thought I had lost.
A little music box is playing
"The Way We Were" and my father's passed out
on the couch, his hand just having released
a roll of Tums.
And then, quick as a freight train,
comes the smell of Aramis and tweed,
and, for some strange reason, ketchup.
The smoke is billowing up from the smokestacks
and moments later figures in Picasso's Guernica
writhe in silent anguish, caught
in the cross-hairs of the business end
of Art. I see the horse's head jutting out
from the mass of flailing limbs – his expression
one of total disbelief, of betrayal,
as if we the viewers must also be partly to blame
to stand there while children are slaughtered.
But what could we have done?
What now can we do?
The next painting comes to us from France:
A lion's tail twitching
in the desert air. What question does he pose
to she who sleeps so peacefully
beneath the Egypt moon? What songs
still echo in the night?

*

Oh to be transported back one night
to the past: Port Authority, 5 a.m.,
the walls lined with sleeping college students
and their enormous backpacks. What do these days
amount to? Is each one like a thread
in some enormous wall-hanging? Is all of it
somehow making sense in a manner detectable only to some
hypothetical outside observer?
I can't believe the water
that drips from my umbrella
was planned, or even coherent at all.
One word is all I need
to replace the wasted moments dropping coins
into payphones late at night.
Oh to be in that 3 dollar guest room
haunted by the smell of ketchup:
Where was it coming from?
What should I do for the rest of my life?
Okay maybe none of this matters, but perhaps
this does: that meaning re-asserts itself
in the clitoral morning after-glow
you see through the parted, swelling curtains:
a light preceding dawn.
The road to the lake is lost in shadows.
I am so sorry.